The Effects of Warning
on Strategic Stability

Brookings Occasional Papers

The Effects of Warning on Strategic Stability

BRUCE G. BLAIR
and
JOHN D. STEINBRUNER

THE BROOKINGS INSTITUTION
Washington, D. C.

Brookings Occasional Papers

THE BROOKINGS INSTITUTION is a private nonprofit organization devoted to research, education, and publication on important issues of domestic and foreign policy. Its principal purpose is to bring knowledge to bear on the major policy problems facing the American people.

On occasion Brookings staff members produce research papers that warrant immediate circulation as contributions to the public debate on current issues of national importance. Because of the speed of their production, these Occasional Papers are not subjected to all of the formal review procedures established for the Institution's research publications, and they may be revised at a later date. As in all Brookings publications, the judgments, conclusions, and recommendations presented in the Papers are solely those of the authors and should not be ascribed to the trustees, officers, or other staff members of the Institution.

Contents

Acknowledgments

The authors appreciate the peer review and valuable suggestions provided by Richard L. Garwin, Ashton B. Carter, Joshua M. Epstein, and Paul B. Stares. Comments from the MITRE Corporation on an early version of the work were also helpful. Ethan Gutmann programmed the model and its graphics; Caroline Lalire edited the manuscript. Research assistance from Sally J. Onesti and administrative support from Charlotte B. Brady and Susan Blanchard are also gratefully acknowledged. Susan L. Woollen prepared the manuscript for typesetting.

Funding for this paper was provided by the Carnegie Corporation of New York and the John D. and Catherine T. MacArthur Foundation. The authors and Brookings are grateful for that support.

John D. Steinbruner is director of Foreign Policy Studies at Brookings. Bruce G. Blair is a senior fellow in the same program.

Introduction

Among its many important effects, the political revolution in central Europe has provided a sharp reminder that international security is as much a state of mind as it is a physical condition. The threat of a Soviet invasion of Western Europe, long hypothesized by Western defense ministries on the basis of a perceived imbalance in inherent conventional force capability, is now acknowledged to be a practical impossibility because shifts in political alignment have been credited. In the wake of that judgment, the force deployments themselves are virtually certain to be reduced, equalized, and disengaged, thereby removing firepower advantage as a threat to international stability. Moreover, though the intrinsic connection is remote, a similar judgment seems to be affecting global strategic deployments. As strategic forces are projected to be reduced to common ceilings by mutual agreement, the fear of preemptive attack on theoretically vulnerable land-based installations appears to be receding more rapidly than the inherent capability that originally inspired it.

This relief from the narrowly focused, obsessive fears that have dominated U.S. security policy for several decades is certainly a constructive development, but unfortunately it is not comprehensively valid. For strategic forces in particular, some subtle interactions between human judgment and physical capability remain potentially dangerous, presenting a security problem that will not be resolved simply by completing the projected agenda of national weapons development and international arms control agreements.

The problem arises from conceivable combinations of events that are undoubtedly improbable but unprecedentedly catastrophic should any of them ever occur. The standards of safety that have evolved for improbable disasters of much smaller magnitude—nuclear reactor meltdowns, for example—have been applied only to peacetime operations and have not been extended to the circumstances of advanced crisis or to the actual initiation of combat operations. To appreciate the implications of this limitation and the dangers that emerge from it

1

requires a substantial revision of standard perspectives on strategic security.

The Standard Strategic Perspective

In the course of four decades of extensive investment in strategic forces, the common understanding of their purposes has depended almost entirely on the idea of deterrence. War is to be prevented by a threat of retaliation that is destructive enough and credible enough to override any expectation of benefit. It is a theory that works for a coherent, calculating decisionmaker, and Americans have become heavily invested in perceiving the opposing strategic forces as if they were the equivalent of rational individuals. Though spirited debates about the elaboration of this logic are still sustained, the principles of a stable strategic balance have nonetheless been established reasonably well. The opposing forces are each to be conceded a bedrock capability to carry out their own assessment of effective retaliation, thereby ensuring the deterrent effect; each is to be denied, however, the ability to destroy the other's retaliatory capability in an initial attack, thereby preventing an incentive to initiate war.

It is conceded that the existing strategic deployments do not fit these principles exactly. The total deployments are larger than reasonably required against accepted retaliatory targets, and the ratio of warheads to strategic force targets is too high. Judgments differ on the details of an ideally stabilized balance, but deployments in the range of 3,000–6,000 total warheads, with the overall ratio of warheads to launchers reduced to, say, a third of its current level (roughly 6:1), would satisfy most of those who hold firm opinions on the question.

Technical calculations of strategic force exchanges reinforce these judgments. Quantitative exchange calculations indicate that existing strategic deployments provide adequate stability in these traditional terms, but that stability could, nonetheless, be improved by judiciously designed reductions down to the level of 3,000 total warheads.[1] Below that number arguments about the most appropriate focus of retaliatory attack would intensify, and prevailing opinion would begin to divide over whether an adequate deterrent capability would be preserved.[2]

The Obscured Problem

This standard strategic perspective involves an obvious simplification that threatens the validity of its conclusions. Strategic forces are not the equivalent of rational individuals. They are in fact large organizations whose internal procedures have considerable difficulty in carrying out the strategic expectations that the standard perspective imposes on them. Retaliation, strictly defined, is particularly demanding, not so much because an initial attack might destroy all the individual weapons required but because it threatens the command system necessary to provide coherent direction. Command system functions can be severely disrupted with a few hundred weapons at most.

This problem has been compounded, moreover, by mission commitments the U.S. and Soviet organizations have developed that are not consistent either with the standard logic of strategic stability or with the practical capability of the weapons at their disposal. Each strategic organization has internally aspired, as a driving priority, to attack the opponent's strategic forces despite its inability to do so decisively. In operational terms, this commitment contradicts the principle of retaliation, since in each instance an attack on the opponent's strategic weapons makes little sense—is indeed a waste of assets—unless it is accomplished preemptively. As a practical matter, the susceptibility of command systems to disruption and the commitment to strategic weapons targeting have created a strong bias for extremely rapid reaction to evidence of impending attack, in effect a launch-on-warning posture for both sides.

The neglected problem of stability emerges from the interaction of the strategic command organizations as they labor to perform their necessary functions under these conditions. The first of these functions, though not often discussed, is their dominant requirement: the organizations must operate strategic forces safely; that is, in a manner that reliably prevents the accidental or unauthorized explosion of even a single weapon. It is questionable that either organization could survive the political repercussions of any major failure of this function, and fortunately both have grasped the imperative. They have evolved sophisticated weapon design principles and operational procedures to preserve effective control with widespread dispersal of weapons and have benefited in that regard from accumulating experience and the process of error correction it allows. On the essential point the record of accomplishment has been perfect to date, a fact that reflects the strong priority given to maintaining strict peacetime control.

That negative requirement is counterposed to the positive function associated with the central strategic purpose. While preserving strict operational control, each strategic organization has also labored to ensure a convincing performance of its wartime missions; that is, it has systematically prepared to carry out the destruction of targets with sufficient aggregate value to deter. Obviously there has never been and can never be any actual experience in carrying out this function, but both strategic organizations have taken it seriously. They maintain a large part of their arsenals in a state capable of operating on short notice and practice the necessary procedures regularly. There is no reason to doubt that undamaged command organizations could deliver most of their weapons to the intended targets on the first attempt. But there is considerable reason to doubt whether a damaged organization could do so, particularly if the damage occurred before the transition from peacetime controls had been accomplished. The fact that command systems can be severely disrupted with very few nuclear weapons creates tension between the peacetime and the wartime functions of a command system and makes the transition between the two states an additional critical function the command system must perform.

The significance of this transition for the contemporary strategic organizations is intensified by the approach they have taken to the operational requirements of deterrence. They have not configured themselves to deliver just a few weapons in retaliation against whatever targets dispersed weapon commanders choose to select. To achieve a comprehensive and efficient coverage of the targets they deem important, both organizations appear to have worked out systematic target assignments for all their deployed weapons on active status. They have also committed themselves to executing attacks on a substantial part of these target assignments, including especially the opposing strategic launchers whose immediate positions can be identified—submarines in port, bombers on bases, and intercontinental ballistic missiles at their known locations. Moreover, at least for the United States, the strategic command system is committed to producing an attack sequence operationally optimized to enhance the penetration of piloted aircraft and to minimize the destruction its own weapons might do to one another.

Because they require a large-scale integration of information, systematic target allocation and attack sequencing entail considerable amounts of time and substantial flows of information. These tasks are performed in advance of any crisis, and the resulting plans cannot be rapidly altered. Since it is unlikely that the planning and communications capability of a command system could survive direct assault well enough to repeat targeting and attack sequencing assignments with anything like the initial efficiency, the effectiveness of retaliation is believed to depend on adherence to previously established plans that are executed before widespread damage to individual weapons has rendered the plans invalid.

This situation places severe transition pressure on the current command systems. Fearful of the disruptive effects of initial damage, both organizations seem to be committed to detecting attack before the definitive evidence of massive damage has accumulated and to disseminating authorization to use weapons, a common targeting plan, and a coordinating time. Were these actions to be taken, the effective power of decision would be decentralized and the reimposition of central control would probably be extremely difficult—particularly given the yet more massive flows of information and confusion that the initial stages of global combat operations would generate.

Since this dissemination of authority is likely to be tantamount to war—in effect replacing strategic assessment by a commitment to executing prepared operations—it must be accomplished without any major error and also without the benefit of accumulating experience. The difficulty of that problem is a much greater strategic danger than has generally been recognized.

The Dynamics Of Warning

The fact that the existing strategic organizations are committed to the virtually irreversible dispersion of central authority in response to evidence of an attack in process makes the stability of the strategic balance turn on the process of warning and imposes severe requirements on that process. A nearly flawless performance is demanded of the sensor networks. They must be sensitive enough to detect signs of transiting weapons yet discriminating enough to recognize spurious signals that only mimic an attack. The information contained in the sensor data must be extracted by an unerring process of filtration. Unassailable rules of evidence must be applied to derive the correct interpretation. Decisionmakers must assimilate the results of this interpretation without introducing their own errors of judgment. The entire process must operate in highly compressed periods of time, no greater than about twenty minutes.

To appreciate the problems posed, it is useful to consider a simple model of it in which all the emotional turbulence that would attend the event has been removed and the process is reduced to realistic rational calculations. That perspective produces difficulty enough, without the need to consider what extreme fear and intense recrimination might add to the situation.

In this simple model the warning system operates as a process of inference using the information derived from sensors to evolve an overall judgment of the probability that an attack is occurring. The process recognizes the traditional types of statistical error—type I, an inference that an attack is not occurring when in fact it is (undetected attack), and type II, an inference that an attack is occurring when in fact it is not (falsely detected attack). The model assigns some probability to each of these errors and with these taken into account changes the overall assessment in reaction to warning sensor outputs according to Bayes's formula for contingent probabilities. Sensor output is sampled at periodic intervals that determine the cycle of judgments for the warning process as a whole. The command systems are assumed to require a probability of attack calculated by this process to be greater than 99 percent before they disseminate authorization for retaliation.

The main effect of this simple model is to shift analytic perspective from outside the warning process (the system designer's perspective) to inside it (the operator's perspective). The discussion of the warning process to date has been predominantly from the designer's perspective. Designers have been instructed, of course, to develop warning systems with extremely low rates of type I and type II, and as best as can be judged from the public record, they have done so reasonably well. Errors do occur with some measurable frequency, but they do not appear to have had any seriously destabilizing result. The overall assessment of the warning process has remained sound and never seems to have approached any point of catastrophe where strategic operations might be dictated by a false inference.

To a degree that is rarely appreciated, however, or at least rarely mentioned, the designer's perspective and the assurances that emanate from it are a result of peacetime experience. There has never been an occasion when one strategic organization seriously began preparing for an immediate attack on the other. Current warning systems have had the opportunity to test their immunity to type II errors only in the context of an overriding presumption that no attack was imminent. That base of experience does not necessarily extend to the circumstances of a serious crisis in which one or both of the main strategic organizations were seriously undertaking the final preparations for attack. Such a situation would trigger alert procedures that would significantly alter normal operational patterns and disrupt the inferences within the opposing warning systems that had been routinized in peacetime. That would probably change the real error rates of the system and would even more likely change the perceived error rates. It would also change the underlying presumption on which the overall assessment is heavily dependent. To explore this unchartered territory without actually experiencing it, it is useful to adopt the operator's perspective inside the warning process.

Operational decisionmakers who carry the burden of controlling strategic forces inevitably depend on their own presumptions. Unlike warning system designers, who can concentrate on their assigned task of extracting empirically valid evidence of a committed attack, operational commanders must consider all the many practicalities that intervene, and they cannot mechanically tie their actions to any sensor system, however highly touted it might be. They will be aware of the inevitable error that human operators introduce into even the most flawless physical systems, and their experiences will have told them that no physical system is flawless in its operation. What they think of any sensor report is inevitably and appropriately weighed by the background information they bring to it attuning them to the inherent possibilities of war and the evolution of the potential adversary's intentions. Whereas the system designer is charged with driving both types of error to statistical margins where they can be considered to have a negligible effect, the operator must take these errors into account as practical possibilities that have extreme significance were they to occur. To the operator a sensor alarm does not automatically mean that an attack is in progress, and the absence of such an alarm does not automatically prove it is not. An integrating judgment is necessary and prior evidence must be brought to bear on the situation.

The application of Bayes's formula for contingent probabilities provides an account of how the required judgment from within the warning system might be made in a disciplined, responsible manner. The process begins with an initial estimate of the probability of attack. This initial subjective expectation is then exposed to confirmatory or contradictory warning reports and is revised using Bayes's formula, which takes into consideration the assumed types I and II error rates of the warning system. Positive warning reports strengthen the decisionmaker's belief that an attack is occurring; negative warning reports (or equivalently, the absence of positive reports indicating attack) weaken it. The *magnitude* of the effect of the reports on the decisionmaker's belief of course depends on his confidence in the warning system, which should correspond to the system's inherent types I and II error rates.

All these prior and posterior *probabilities* are strictly *subjective* in the Bayesian model; they are opinions that exist in the minds of individuals. Data supplied by warning sensors do not objectively validate the probabilities but merely enable existing opinion to be revised logically by the successive application of Bayes's formula. The formula permits decisionmakers to assimilate evidence acquired by space- and ground-based surveillance in a way that ensures coherence and consistency in the evolution of expectations.

There is an important sense in which Bayesian probabilities can be considered "objective," however. As more sensor data become available, the posterior probabilities of individuals with initially disparate prior probabilities will converge. Despite the Bayesian denial of objectively warranted degrees of belief, and the espousal of the view that all prior and posterior probabilities are strictly individual opinion— statements of personal probabilities—intersubjective agreement will be reached eventually so long as sufficient data are brought to bear on opinion. The weight of initial opinion declines and eventually dissipates completely as it is combined with the accumulating data outputs of the tactical warning network.[3]

Reassuring Illustrations

For the sake of illustration let us assume the tactical warning system has a constant error rate of 5 percent for each type of error. Suppose the warning system indicates that an attack is being launched. From a non-Bayesian perspective that ignores context, particularly the subjective state of the command system, and focuses exclusively on design specifications of the tactical warning system, the alarm is credible because the system is unlikely to sound an alarm when an attack is not occurring. The likelihood of its ringing the alarm by mistake is only 5 percent. Suppose the system takes a second look at the environment and confirms its earlier report. According to non-Bayesian logic, an attack is definitely under way because the tactical warning system is extremely unlikely to sound two false alarms in a row. The likelihood of that happening is 5 percent × 5 percent = one-fourth of 1 percent, or 0.0025. This non-Bayesian calculation suggests that two positive readings from the tactical warning system would strongly justify the dissemination of authorization to retaliate.

But a Bayesian rational commander would not function in a contextual vacuum. Such a commander would take a broader view of the situation and would draw the opposite conclusion under many circumstances. The same warning reports from the identical system can lead to a different conclusion, because a Bayesian commander does not rely on them to the exclusion of prior information, or opinion. Instead, the Bayesian commander combines the reports with prior expectations of attack to produce a revised expectation.[4]

Suppose the initial subjective expectation of attack was very low— for instance, 0.001, a prior probability consistent with normal peacetime tensions. After receiving the first attack warning from the sensor network, a rationally calculating commander, upon applying Bayes's rule of inductive inference, will revise his personal subjective probability from 0.001 to 0.019 (see table 1). Although the commander's degree of belief in the proposition that an attack is under way will increase nearly twentyfold, the revised probability remains very low in absolute terms. After taking a second reading of the warning system, which confirms the earlier positive indication of attack, the commander will undergo another change of opinion, revising his probability from 0.019 to 0.265. He thus will remain highly skeptical that an attack is under way in spite of two back-to-back reports of attack. His implicit subjective estimate that *both* alarms are *false* is about 73 percent (1.000 minus 0.265), a calculation that stands in stark contrast to the earlier non-Bayesian calculation that the probability of receiving two successive false alarms is only one-fourth of 1 percent (0.0025). The Bayesian calculation, unlike the non-Bayesian estimate, would not strongly justify the dissemination of authorization to retaliate. On the contrary, it would reject the hypothesis that an attack is under way, on the grounds of insufficient evidence. Additional evidence of attack is necessary to tip the scales in favor of the hypothesis. To be precise, a third positive alarm would raise the probability to 0.873, and a fourth would push it to 0.992, which crosses the presumed threshold for ordering retaliation.

In this illustration the feasibility of a launch-on-warning posture is questionable because four cycles of judgment are needed to establish a strong belief that an attack is under way, while ballistic missiles with short flight times over intercontinental range allow for at most two cycles associated with dual-sensor (satellite infrared and ground radar) technology.

Its feasibility is far less doubtful in crisis circumstances, however, when the initial expectation of attack is stronger and the necessary cycles of judgment are therefore fewer. Table 1 illustrates this relationship. The first column displays a range of degrees of belief in the prospect of enemy attack that a command system might have before receiving attack information. The columns to the right of it show how these initial expectations would be altered according to Bayes's formula after the command system receives one or more positive reports of attack from the tactical warning system, knowing the inherent error rate of the system (assumed to be a constant error rate of 5 percent for types I and II errors).

As the table clearly suggests, the effect of tactical warning information depends on the expectations of the commanders receiving it, and Bayesian commanders whose initial expectations of attack exceed 20 percent will approach the certainty ($p > 0.990$) that presumably would

Table 1. Initial and Revised Expectations of Attack (Given Attack Warning) Assuming a Warning System with 5 Percent Types I and II Error Rates

	Revised estimate given attack warning					
Initial		*Number of positive warning reports:*				
estimate[a]	*1*	*2*	*3*	*4*	*5*	*6*
0.0001	0.002	0.035	0.407	0.929	0.996	1.000
0.001	0.019	0.265	0.873	0.992	1.000	
0.01	0.161	0.785	0.986	0.999	1.000	
0.05	0.500	0.950	0.999	1.000		
0.10	0.679	0.976	0.999	1.000		
0.20	0.826	0.989	0.999	1.000		
0.30	0.891	0.994	1.000			
0.40	0.927	0.996	1.000			
0.50	0.950	0.997	1.000			
0.60	0.966	0.998	1.000			
0.70	0.978	0.999	1.000			
0.80	0.987	0.999	1.000			
0.90	0.994	1.000				
0.95	0.997	1.000				
0.99	0.999	1.000				
0.999	1.000					
0.9999	1.000					

a. Degree of belief in the hypothesis "an attack is under way."

be demanded to trigger retaliation after two cycles of judgment that each have positive indication of attack. Two attack alarms in succession, which correspond to the dual-detection technology of missile warning systems, are sufficient data to infer that the enemy has indeed launched an attack. Lower in the columns, the table shows, moreover, that if the commander enters the sequence of warning system readings with a very high expectation of attack ($p > 0.840$), then a solitary alarm will drive it over the threshold ($p > 0.990$) in a single cycle of judgment. The table thus confirms the feasibility of launch on warning in situations in which the command system is already apprehensive about an enemy attack when the attack alarm goes off. These are of course crisis situations, not normal peacetime conditions.

Initial apprehension is a double-edged sword, however. Although it renders launch on warning a feasible and rational response to positive indications of attack, it also renders the command system more

Table 2. Initial and Revised Expectations of Attack (Given No Attack Warning) Assuming a Warning System with 5 Percent Types I and II Error Rates

Initial estimate[a]	Revised estimate given no attack warning					
	Number of negative warning reports:					
	1	*2*	*3*	*4*	*5*	*6*
0.0001	0.000					
0.001	0.000					
0.01	0.001	0.000				
0.05	0.003	0.000				
0.10	0.006	0.000				
0.20	0.013	0.001	0.000			
0.30	0.022	0.001	0.000			
0.40	0.034	0.002	0.000			
0.50	0.050	0.003	0.000			
0.60	0.073	0.004	0.000			
0.70	0.109	0.006	0.000			
0.80	0.174	0.011	0.001	0.000		
0.90	0.320	0.024	0.001	0.000		
0.95	0.500	0.050	0.003	0.000		
0.99	0.839	0.215	0.014	0.001		
0.999	0.981	0.735	0.127	0.008	0.000	
0.9999	0.998	0.965	0.593	0.071	0.004	0.000

a. Degree of belief in the hypothesis "an attack is under way."

susceptible to the effects of false positive indications of attack. In the last illustration given above, a solitary alarm sends an apprehensive commander over the edge in a single cycle—a prior expectation of 0.84 goes to 0.99 upon receipt of one report. The commander's personal subjective estimate that the alarm is false is only 1 percent (1.000 minus 0.990), yet according to design specifications the false alarm error rate is five times higher because the type II (falsely detected attack) error rate is assumed to be 5 percent. An anxious command system is thus prone to overreaction to preliminary indications of attack. It should wait for the second report, since the indications are likely (95 percent) to be negative if no attack is actually occurring, in which case the commander's subjective expectation will revert back to 0.84 and his impulse to disseminate authorization to retaliate will be checked.

Table 2 illustrates the effects of negative warning reports on prior subjective expectations. The first column shows a range of degrees of belief in the prospect of enemy attack that a command system might have before receiving attack information. The columns to the right of it show how these initial expectations would be altered according to Bayes's formula after the command system receives one or more negative reports of attack from the tactical warning system, knowing the inherent error rate of the system (assumed to be a constant error rate of 5 percent for types I and II errors).

The table clearly suggests that the effect of warning system information depends on the expectations of the commanders receiving it and that Bayesian commanders whose initial expectations of attack are very high will remain very apprehensive after one cycle of judgment with negative indication of attack—for instance, 0.990 goes to 0.839. After two cycles of judgment, each with negative indication of attack, their fears will abate considerably—for instance, 0.990 goes to 0.215 after two iterations. Apprehension thus lasts for a while when commanders enter the sequence of warning system readings with very high subjective expectations of attack. Negative reports do not totally discredit their belief that an attack is under way, even though the assumed type I (undetected attack) error rate is only 5 percent. Whereas the design specifications of the tactical warning system suggest there is a 5 percent chance that the system's initial report will provide negative attack indications when an attack is actually occurring, and a one-fourth percent chance that it will file two such erroneous reports in a row, a Bayesian commander implicitly estimates the chances at 84 percent and 22 percent, respectively, if that person entered the sequence of readings with an initial expectation of attack of 99 percent.

The overall performance reflected in tables 1 and 2 suggests that a warning system with a constant error rate of 5 percent for type I and type II errors is serviceable, though just barely, for supporting the current rapid reaction or launch-on-warning postures of the U.S. and Soviet strategic establishments. Dual-sensor technology allows for two cycles of judgment before launch on warning is authorized, which is both necessary and sufficient to limit the scope for gross misjudgment in the decision process within the most plausible range of circumstances. The warning system appears to adequately serve the basic aims of the command system: positive and negative control.

Regarding positive control, launch on warning is a feasible option in the event of enemy attack except in the implausible circumstance of a surprise attack in peacetime, when commanders least expect an attack and hence require more than two readings from the tactical warning system to become convinced. Two readings are sufficient for the more plausible circumstances of a superpower crisis, when commanders become attuned to the possibility of war and grow more apprehensive as the situation deteriorates. As table 1 indicates, an initial subjective expectation of 20 percent will be revised to 99 percent in round numbers (0.989 to be precise) after two cycles of judgment, each with positive indication of attack. It seems reasonable to suppose that commanders' initial expectations in the midst of an intense confrontation would approach or surpass the 20 percent level necessary to ensure virtual certitude after two successive tactical warning alarms.[5]

Regarding negative control, two cycles of judgment that each have negative attack indications will, as table 2 shows, produce a sharp downward moderation of apprehension if commanders enter the sequence of warning readings with a very high expectation of attack. Dual-sensor technology thus helps ensure that the preconceptions of commanders are exposed to sufficient tactical warning evidence to correct their biases. A strong predisposition to authorize attack in anticipation of imminent enemy attack will slacken enormously after two successive negative reports are received from the warning system. Since the command system can afford to wait for two such assessments before committing to its reaction, the scope for miscalculation is greatly reduced. The dangers appear to be mitigated.

The primary apparent drawback of the warning system outlined here is that one cannot safely assume that two successive alarms would sound in the event of attack, or that two successive negative reports would be issued in the event of no attack. There is a small chance that the tactical warning system would file a different combination of reports, given its 5 percent rate of types I and II errors. The probability that it gives a positive reading twice in a row in the event of attack is 95 percent × 95 percent, or approximately 90 percent. In consequence, there is a 10 percent chance that it fails to provide the two successive positive attack indications necessary to facilitate launch on warning under the range of prior expectations that seem most plausible under crisis circumstances. Similarly, the probability that the system gives a negative reading twice in a row in the event of no attack is also 95 percent × 95 percent, or 90 percent. In consequence, there is a significant chance (10 percent) that a very high expectation of attack will not decline as steeply as the benign state of nature would warrant.

These apparent liabilities would be mitigated if, as many system designers believe, the deployed warning system was less error prone than our analysis assumes. Typical estimates of the inherent error rates of the U.S. tactical warning network are so minuscule as to be negligible. The type II (false alarm) rate in particular is generally deemed to be vanishingly small. The MITRE Corporation, for example, which plays an importent role in designing and evaluating the U.S. tactical warning system, noted in a memorandum that a 5 percent false alarm rate corresponds to five false alarms per eight-hour duty shift in the operational system, based on an average false alarm duration of 300 seconds.[6] In the words of the authors of the memorandum: "In the fairy tale, the little boy who called 'wolf' too often got eaten; here his sensor system would never have been bought in the first place." The authors assume that the system produces only ten false alarms a year, each with a duration of 300 seconds, which corresponds to a type II error rate of about 0.0001. They do not choose to contest the assumption of a type I (undetected attack) error rate of 5 percent. This assumption perhaps goes unchallenged for two reasons: the blindness of some U.S. sensors to missiles launched from certain areas of the Arctic Ocean, and the frequent downtime experienced by operational sensors because of equipment malfunction, routine maintenance, and periodic modernization efforts.

For the sake of illustration, let us accept the MITRE assumptions to show the effect of warning system information on the expectations of commanders. We assume a tactical warning system with a constant error rate of 5 percent for type I (undetected attack) and one one-hundredth percent (0.0001) for type II (falsely detected attack) errors. Column 1 of table 3 shows a range of prior subjective estimates, and the columns to the right show the revised estimates after one or more readings of the warning system are taken. The table clearly suggests that the effects of tactical warning on commanders' expectations are dramatic. Initial beliefs carry little weight in the calculation. Tactical warning evidence carries overwhelming weight, swamping the influence of prior subjective opinion on posterior belief in a single cycle of judgment.

Table 3. Initial and Revised Expectations of Attack (Given Attack Warning) Assuming a Warning System with 5 Percent Type I and 0.0001 Type II Error Rates

	Revised estimate given attack warning	
	Number of positive warning reports:	
Initial estimate[a]	1	2
0.0001	0.487	1.000
0.001	0.905	1.000
0.01	0.990	1.000
0.05	0.998	1.000
0.10	0.997	1.000
0.20	1.000	
0.30	1.000	
0.40	1.000	
0.50	1.000	
0.60	1.000	
0.70	1.000	
0.80	1.000	
0.90	1.000	
0.95	1.000	
0.99	1.000	
0.999	1.000	

a. Degree of belief in the hypothesis "an attack is under way"

These calculations imply that effective rapid reaction is feasible under all conditions and scenarios including surprise attack in peacetime. Even when the initial expectation of attack is extremely low, positive indication of attack will produce a sharp upward adjustment in a single cycle of judgment. Still, there is a small chance (5 percent) that the tactical warning system would not detect an attack on the first scan. Furthermore, if command system procedures require two successive alarms before authorizing retaliation, as prudence would dictate, then the type I (undetected attack) error rate has two opportunities to manifest itself. The probability that the warning system gives a positive reading twice in a row in the event of attack is 95 percent × 95 percent, or approximately 90 percent. In consequence, there is a 10 percent chance that it fails to provide the two successive positive alarms.

On the other hand, if the criterion for authorizing launch is simply that virtual certitude ($p > 0.99$) exists after two readings of the tactical

Table 4. Initial and Revised Expectations of Attack (Given No Attack Warning) Assuming a Warning System with a 5 Percent Type I and 0.0001 Type II Error Rates

Initial estimate[a]	Revised estimate given no attack warning				
	Number of negative warning reports:				
	1	2	3	4	5
0.001	0.000				
0.01	0.000				
0.10	0.001	0.000			
0.20	0.012	0.001	0.000		
0.30	0.021	0.001	0.000		
0.40	0.032	0.002	0.000		
0.50	0.048	0.002	0.000		
0.60	0.070	0.004	0.000		
0.70	0.104	0.006	0.000		
0.80	0.167	0.010	0.000		
0.90	0.310	0.022	0.001	0.000	
0.99	0.832	0.198	0.012	0.001	0.000
0.999	0.980	0.714	0.111	0.006	0.000

a. Degree of belief in the hypothesis "an attack is under way."

warning system are taken, then both readings need not be positive in some circumstances. It is readily seen from tables 3 and 4 that one positive reading will suffice when commanders enter the sequence with an expectation of 17 percent or higher, as well they might in crisis circumstances. If either the first or second report provides positive indication of attack, the commander's posterior probability will exceed 99 percent despite exposure to a negative report during one of the cycles of judgment. A solitary alarm will boost an already apprehensive commander to such a high level of expectation that a solitary negative report will not drive his expectation below the triggering threshold. In this case, rapid reaction is more feasible. The type I (undetected attack) error rate must manifest itself twice in a row to prevent a launch decision, and the probability of this happening is very remote (5 percent × 5 percent, or one-fourth percent).

Not only do the MITRE assumptions inspire confidence in the feasibility of a rapid reaction posture under a wider range of circumstances, but they also allay concern about the susceptibility of the command system to miscalculation stemming from false alarms. The type II (falsely detected attack) error rate is vanishingly small (0.0001). If the criterion for launch authorization is virtual certitude after two readings, then an apprehensive commander with an initial expectation of 17 percent or higher will be driven above the triggering threshold by a single false alarm received during either cycle of judgment. But the chances of this happening are remote. The probability that the warning system will *not* issue a false alarm on either scan is 99.99 percent × 99.99 percent, or 99.98 percent. Thus the probability that it will mistakenly issue the fateful report is only 0.02 percent (0.0002). If the criterion for launch authorization is two positive alarms in succession, then the chances of mistaken inference are still lower. The probability of issuing two false alarms in a row is 0.01 percent × 0.01 percent, or 0.0001 percent (0.00000001).

These calculations help explain the prevailing confidence in the stability of an international security arrangement based on opposing strategic forces operationally committed to rapid reaction in response to direct evidence of immediate attack. The historical record seems to reinforce this theoretical confidence in the viability and safety of operational practices that at first blush strike many observers as too tenuous to underwrite deterrence and too catalytic to avoid fatal mistakes. Although a small theoretical chance exists that launch on warning could not be exercised successfully in a real attack, both military establishments prudently credit the adversary with the capability and express cautious optimism about their own capability. They can also cite the historical record to contest the view that launch on warning puts the nuclear postures on a dangerous hair trigger. Dual-sensor technology reduces the theoretical odds of accidental war to negligible proportions, and the fact that false alarms produced by the operational U.S. warning system have never even resulted in the notification of the national command authorities, let alone induced nuclear release deliberations, provides empirical substantiation of the theoretical claim.

Reasons for Doubt

Closer investigation of the difficulty of the tactical warning problem, however, using the Bayesian model as the main tool of analysis, reveals serious grounds for doubting the standard strategic assessment. Doubts begin with the elementary observation that the frequency of false alarms is a relative measure that varies with the amount of time one allows for them to appear. The incidence of false alarm thus rises as the duration of crisis increases. A type II error rate of 0.0001 per 300-second interval (the nominal duration of a warning report period), for instance, means that a false alarm rarely occurs in any given five-minute period, but that one will occur with statistical regularity every thirty-five days. A false alarm is virtually bound to arise during a month-long crisis. A crisis that lasts for one week stands a 20 percent chance of suffering a warning failure of the second type.

Another elementary observation is that the nuclear decision process involves a *group* of individuals. Launch on warning is not the decision of one person, and the decision does not stem from the inductive inference of any single person in the warning system. The decision is collective, and it presupposes a consensus among key military and civilian actors on the question whether or not an enemy attack has been launched.

This need for intersubjective agreement presents a special difficulty. Because the actors occupy different positions within the warning network and command system, they are unlikely to hold uniform subjective expectations of attack before receiving tactical warning information; moreover, their disparate initial beliefs are exposed to different levels of tactical information at different times and rates.

To illustrate the difficulties of synchronizing a process of collective judgment, consider the relation between the North American Aerospace Defense Command (NORAD) and the U.S. president. The former enters the sequence of tactical warning readings with initial expectations of attack that at times surely differ from those of the national command authorities, given their dissimilar perceptual filters and accesses to strategic warning, political intelligence, and special sources of assessment.

The differences are presumably small in peacetime. A bolt-out-of-the-blue attack would catch almost everyone by surprise, a psychological reaction implying that a very low expectation of attack permeates the command system. Subjective expectations are likely to diverge in crisis circumstances, however. It is characteristic of crisis that ambiguity surrounds the intentions of an adversary and that cleavages of perception develop within the command system. The adversary's behavior supports a range of alternative explanations and threat estimates. This diversity gives rise to disparate opinions within the command system on the likelihood that the crisis will lead to enemy attack. Achieving internal consensus to mesh the beliefs at the apex of government with the projections of the military establishment is one of the chief dramas of crisis management. Mutually consistent expectations among the many political and military actors in the command system may prove difficult to establish and maintain during a crisis.[7]

Decentralized processing of tactical information further hampers the convergence of collective judgment. The NORAD organization, for example, receives tactical warning information and begins processing the data before the national command authorities are even notified. It could complete two cycles of judgment before the national level receives its initial notification. Although NORAD might converge on a clear judgment after multiple exposures to tactical information, national commanders might treat NORAD's summary interpretation as a single positive alarm to be processed in a single cycle of judgment. Convergence on clear judgment thus proceeds more slowly at the national level. Several parallel processes of Bayesian adjustment, each converging on independent judgments at a different pace, must be reconciled in a very short time. Consensus might emerge, but not as readily as it would if the various actors shared the same initial expectations and simultaneously processed the identical tactical warning information.

While Bayesian calculations will eventually overcome disparate beliefs and converge on clear consensual judgment, given sufficient cycles of judgment and reasonably accurate tactical sensors, the fact that launch on warning restricts the number of judgment cycles to two at the most means that initial subjective expectations often strongly determine judgment at the point of its forced truncation. The problem of intersubjective agreement aside, it is evident that *accurate* prior estimates facilitate convergence within the small number of cycles that current strategic force reaction times allow.

But it is also evident that the initial predictions of commanders rest on very "soft" indicators of enemy intent. Strategic warning is a notoriously dubious source of knowledge about the future. This then is another characteristic of a crisis. Subjective expectations of attack undergo significant change under the influence of low-grade strategic warning. And the fact that the exposure of these suspect expectations to "hard" tactical warning evidence is too limited under the time constraints of currently planned strategic operations to wash out their biasing effect on posterior opinion raises troubling questions.

The truncation of Bayesian learning after only two cycles of judgment in effect transfers a large part of the burden of proof from tactical to strategic warning systems. Although tactical warning offers or withholds the increment of certainty needed to carry commanders across the threshold for authorizing retaliation, this increment builds on the baseline certainty represented by initial expectations stemming from strategic warning. Initial belief acts as as a pedestal that, together with the marginal certainty derived from tactical information, can boost the total certainty to the release flashpoint. In this sense the accuracy of initial belief is crucial to the outcome. The overall quality of Bayesian inference in these cases cannot be better than the quality of one of its essential constituent parts (initial belief). Initial subjective expectations constitute the weakest link in its train of logic, and the train is only as strong as this particular link when the number of allowable adjustments are few.[8]

A hypothetical case in point is a situation in which an initial expectation of 50 percent jumps to 99 percent after positive attack indications are received from the tactical warning system. If the two tactical alarms were false (from table 5, the risk of this happening is 1 percent), then the inaccurate initial expectation is no less responsible than the tactical warning system for producing the mistaken conclusion that an enemy attack is under way. Had the prior belief been less apprehensive (more accurate in its correspondence with the true state of nature), the certainty that induces nuclear response would not have been reached. For instance, a prior expectation of 1 percent goes to 45 percent after two positive indications are received in succession. This comparison shows that initial expectation based on strategic warning can be a *decisive* parameter.

Rapid reaction or literal launch on warning in such cases is no less susceptible to the effects of strategic misjudgment than preemption is. Both policies lean on the thin reed of accurate strategic warning. Contrary to prevalent opinion, launch on warning, though triggered by tactical indications, does not avoid the problem of unreliable strategic warning usually associated with preemption. The option cannot divorce itself from this problem unless the error rates of the tactical warning system are vanishingly small, in which case initial expectations carry negligible weight in Bayesian computations over one or two cycles of judgment.

The use of *constant* and *low* error rates for all situations is a standard but dubious assumption. That error rates attributed to operational tactical warning systems reflect performance realized in peacetime operations raises the question whether the rates in crisis circumstances might be substantially worse.

There are evident grounds for believing, or better fearing, that one of the effects of crisis might well be a degradation of both type I and type II error rates. The potential rate of unusual observations would increase as strategic systems under surveillance began to change their peacetime routines. The adversary's dispersal of strategic forces over wider geographic areas in increasing variety and numbers—for instance, the alerting of cruise missiles on aircraft and submarines—would present an unusual deployment pattern that tactical warning networks had never before encountered. The normal rate of observational error might well increase as the scale and the scope of observations expanded, and the interpretive logic used would be forced to depart from accustomed routine. Thus the error rates assumed in tables 1 and 2 (5 percent rates of types I and II errors) and tables 5–8 (10 or 25 percent rate of type I and 10 or 25 percent rate of type II error), while undoubtedly too high for peacetime operations, might well be more realistic for crisis circumstances. It is in any case difficult to prove the contrary.

In the realm of ideas, as opposed to firm conclusions, *a crisis can be defined in precisely these terms*: one of its distinguishing features is that the types I and II error rates of the tactical warning system rapidly degrade. A crisis not only ushers in the proverbial "fog of crisis" symptomatic of error-prone strategic warning but also ushers in a "fog of war" arising from an analogous deterioration of tactical warning. Again, a simple explanation underlies this effect. Warning systems that have been calibrated for peacetime surveillance and seldom exercised in crisis circumstances have not evolved through trial and error a proved effective repertory of observational routines to deal with those unusual circumstances.

Deeper Reflections

With these doubts in mind, it is useful to develop a more rigorous conception of the discontinuous deterioration of intelligence that plagues the transition from peacetime to crisis environments. In stable peacetime environments, an intelligence system learns through trial and error to monitor and interpret the adversary's strategic disposition. The system experiments with alternative configurations of technologies and procedures, focusing on selected critical variables of the adversary's operations, and gradually achieves partial successes in keeping the variables within proper limits. It then *retains* the successful trial designs while improving what is still unsatisfactory. The stable environment permits use to be made of partial adaptation, and further experimentation produces yet more successes. This gradual accumulation of adaptations and concomitant weeding out of unsuccessful routines are the result of repetitive, experiential learning whose specific effect is to drive down the error rates for the environment to which the warning network is adapting, namely a peacetime environment.

To illustrate the process, suppose that the peacetime operation of a single sensor system involves four independent components: sensor, communications, computer analysis, and human operators, each with a type II error rate of 10 percent for every 300-second report period. Through trial and error, the system evolves a repertory of responses to positive attack indications which ensures that an attack alarm will never be sounded unless all four components are mutually consistent and self-confirmatory. All four must simultaneously indicate an attack. Cross-checking and other diagnostic procedures ensure that no positive attack report is issued if the readings from any of the four components are negative during a report interval. Furthermore, at the end of a given 300-second report period, all four components are reset for the next cycle of readings, so that no previous attack indications, positive or negative, spill over into subsequent periods. In this case of continuous recycling, the probability of a systemic type II error—defined as a simultaneous type II error in all four components in the same report period—is only 0.0001, which corresponds to one false alarm every 833.33 hours (about once every thirty-five days). This false alarm rate for a single sensor system (infrared or radar) is identical to the MITRE Corporation's assumption and is consistent with factual knowledge of peacetime performance.

Suppose, however, that one of the effects of crisis is the lowering of the adaptive capacity of the warning system's repertory. Human fatigue, changes in surveillance configuration, an increase in the potential rate and scope of observation, the departure of interpretive logic from accustomed routine, and other unusual factors present a unique situation to which the warning-command system has not adapted through the standard learning process. The result is a slower accumulation of trial successes and a stronger retention of trial errors. A system that proved nimble in its usual environment suddenly becomes clumsy in an unfamiliar situation.

The frequency and duration of both types of error increase and might even take a quantum jump. The incidence of systemic type II errors, for example, could be dramatically higher if component type II errors—for instance, the misreading of warning output by human operators—were carried over from one report period to the next. A simple calculation shows that the temporary retention of component type II error could produce a systemic false alarm approximately every fifty minutes on average, instead of every thirty-five days. In other words, the false alarm rate of the tactical warning system changes from 0.0001 per five-minute report period to 0.1 per period, a degradation of three orders of magnitude.[9]

The error rates of the warning systems might deteriorate still more if the crisis erupts into war and the networks sustain damage before or during the release of strategic forces.

The prospect of sudden nonlinear degradation of warning performance caused by rapid environmental change has systematic implications for Bayesian inference and hence for the rapid reaction posture of current strategic forces. A nonlinear change in error rates either severely impedes Bayesian convergence on clear judgment or causes expectations to converge too rapidly, depending on whether the error rate change actually registers with the actors in the command system.

If there is a corresponding degradation of internal confidence in warning performance—for example, *case 1,* in which an increase in warning system error leads to a corresponding correction of the error rate assumptions used in the actors' calculations—then the result of error rate change is a dramatic diminution of the impact of tactical

Table 5. Initial and Revised Expectations of Attack (Given Attack Warning) Assuming a Warning System with 10 Percent Types I and II Error Rates

Initial estimate[a]	Revised estimate given attack warning							
	Number of positive warning reports:							
	1	2	3	4	5	6	7	8
0.0001	0.001	0.008	0.068	0.396	0.855	0.982	0.998	1.000
0.001	0.009	0.075	0.422	0.868	0.983	0.998	1.000	
0.01	0.083	0.450	0.880	0.985	0.998	1.000		
0.05	0.321	0.810	0.975	0.997	1.000			
0.10	0.500	0.900	0.988	0.999	1.000			
0.20	0.692	0.953	0.995	0.999	1.000			
0.30	0.794	0.972	0.997	1.000				
0.40	0.857	0.982	0.998	1.000				
0.50	0.900	0.988	0.999	1.000				
0.60	0.931	0.992	0.999					
0.70	0.955	0.995	0.999					
0.80	0.973	0.997						
0.90	0.998	0.999						
0.95	0.994	0.999						
0.99	0.999	1.000						
0.999	1.000							
0.9999	1.000							

a. Degree of belief in the hypothesis "an attack is under way."

warning information on expectations of attack. Initial subjective expectations are slower to change after exposure to this information. Successive readings of warning system output do not readily converge on a clear judgment.

If there is no corresponding degradation of confidence—for example, *case 2*, in which commanders continue to use the peacetime error rates in their calculations despite an actual degradation in warning system error rates—the effect is to accelerate convergence on a judgment that credits tactical warning information with more validity than it deserves. In this circumstance subjective expectations of attack are overdetermined by tactical information.

Case 1

Tables 5 and 6 illustrate case 1 when the error rate assumptions used in commanders' calculations have been changed to 10 percent for

Table 6. Initial and Revised Expectations of Attack (Given No Attack Warning) Assuming a Warning System with 10 Percent Types I and II Error Rates

Initial estimate[a]	Revised estimate given no attack warning						
	Number of negative warning reports:						
	1	*2*	*3*	*4*	*5*	*6*	*7*
0.0001	0.000						
0.001	0.000						
0.01	0.001	0.000					
0.05	0.006	0.001					
0.10	0.012	0.001					
0.20	0.027	0.003					
0.30	0.045	0.005	0.001				
0.40	0.069	0.008	0.001				
0.50	0.100	0.012	0.001				
0.60	0.143	0.018	0.002				
0.70	0.206	0.028	0.003				
0.80	0.308	0.047	0.005	0.001			
0.90	0.500	0.100	0.012	0.001			
0.95	0.679	0.190	0.025	0.003			
0.99	0.917	0.550	0.120	0.015	0.002		
0.999	0.991	0.925	0.578	0.132	0.017	0.002	
0.9999	0.999	0.992	0.932	0.604	0.145	0.018	0.002

a. Degree of belief in the hypothesis "an attack is under way."

types I and II errors. Tables 7 and 8 assume an even greater decline in confidence in warning performance due perhaps to damage suffered by the warning networks: the actual and assumed errors rates are 25 percent. The format of the presentation is the same as in the previous tables.

These data demonstrate that reduced performance of the system (matched by reduced subjective confidence vested in the system) increases the number of cycles required for the Bayesian commander to adjust the initial expectation. Tables 5 and 7 show that many cycles of judgment that each have positive indication of attack are necessary before judgment becomes clear enough to support the decision about whether or not to disseminate authorization to retaliate. Since current strategic postures appear to permit only two readings before a decision must be rendered, the coherent operations are virtually infeasible in the circumstances reflected in table 7, and feasible only in a narrow band of circumstances reflected in table 5 (when commanders enter

Table 7. Initial and Revised Expectations of Attack (Given Attack Warning) Assuming a Warning System with 25 Percent Types I and II Error Rates

Revised estimate given attack warning

Number of positive warning reports:

Initial estimate[a]	1	2	3	4	5	6	7	8	9	10	11	12	13	14	15	16
0.0001	0.000+	0.001	0.003	0.008	0.024	0.068	0.179	0.396	0.663	0.855	0.947	0.982	0.994	0.998	0.999	1.000
0.001	0.003	0.009	0.026	0.075	0.196	0.422	0.686	0.868	0.952	0.983	0.994	0.998	0.999			
0.01	0.029	0.083	0.214	0.450	0.711	0.880	0.957	0.985	0.995	0.998	0.999					
0.05	0.136	0.321	0.587	0.810	0.927	0.975	0.991	0.997	0.999	1.000						
0.10	0.250	0.500	0.750	0.900	0.964	0.988	0.996	0.999								
0.20	0.429	0.692	0.871	0.953	0.984	0.995	0.998	0.999								
0.30	0.563	0.794	0.920	0.972	0.990	0.997	0.999									
0.40	0.667	0.857	0.947	0.982	0.994	0.998	0.999									
0.50	0.750	0.900	0.964	0.988	0.996	0.998										
0.60	0.818	0.931	0.976	0.992	0.997	0.999										
0.70	0.875	0.955	0.984	0.995	0.998	0.999										
0.80	0.923	0.973	0.991	0.997	0.999											
0.90	0.964	0.988	0.996	0.999												
0.95	0.983	0.994	0.998	0.999												
0.99	0.997	0.999														
0.999	1.000															

a. Degree of belief in the hypothesis "an attack is under way."

Table 8. Initial and Revised Expectations of Attack (Given No Attack Warning) Assuming a Warning System with 25 Percent Types I and II Error Rates

Revised estimate given no attack warning

Initial estimate[a]	Number of negative warning reports:													
	1	*2*	*3*	*4*	*5*	*6*	*7*	*8*	*9*	*10*	*11*	*12*	*13*	*14*
0.0001	0.000													
0.001	0.000													
0.01	0.003	0.001	0.000											
0.05	0.017	0.006	0.002	0.001	0.000									
0.10	0.036	0.012	0.004	0.001	0.000									
0.20	0.077	0.027	0.009	0.003	0.001	0.000								
0.30	0.125	0.045	0.016	0.005	0.002	0.001								
0.40	0.182	0.069	0.024	0.008	0.003	0.001								
0.50	0.250	0.100	0.036	0.012	0.004	0.001								
0.60	0.333	0.143	0.053	0.018	0.006	0.002	0.001							
0.70	0.438	0.206	0.080	0.028	0.010	0.003	0.001							
0.80	0.571	0.308	0.129	0.047	0.016	0.005	0.002	0.001						
0.90	0.750	0.500	0.250	0.100	0.036	0.012	0.004	0.001						
0.95	0.864	0.679	0.413	0.190	0.073	0.025	0.009	0.003	0.001					
0.99	0.971	0.917	0.786	0.550	0.289	0.120	0.043	0.015	0.005	0.002	0.001			
0.999	0.997	0.991	0.974	0.925	0.804	0.578	0.314	0.132	0.048	0.017	0.006	0.002	0.001	
0.9999	0.999	0.997	0.992	0.976	0.932	0.821	0.604	0.337	0.145	0.053	0.016	0.006	0.002	0.001

a. Degree of belief in the hypothesis "an attack is under way."

the sequence of tactical warning readings with a high [$p > 0.590$] initial expectation of attack). This limited feasibility is further qualified by the fact that the tactical warning system assumed in table 5 is somewhat prone to issue a negative report in circumstances of actual attack. Given its assumed type I error rate of 10 percent, detecting the attack on each of two successive scans of the environment is not ensured. The likelihood of this happening is in fact 81 percent (90 percent × 90 percent). For the warning system reflected in table 7, which assumes a type I error rate of 25 percent, the likelihood of getting two positive attack indications in a row is only 56 percent (75 percent × 75 percent), though the point is moot, since two cycles of judgment that each have positive indications are insufficient to reach a conclusive judgment.

As an excursion on these Bayesian computations involving relatively high error rates, it is useful to note a significant difference between strategic delivery systems in the type of burden they impose on warning systems. Ballistic missiles with a thirty-minute flight time over intercontinental range allow for only two cycles of judgment, yet a large number of ballistic missile launchers would give relatively unambiguous warning to satellite infrared sensors and thus fairly rapid convergence of judgment on detection of attack. For this reason a type II error under crisis conditions would be very dangerous even though a single false alarm would not drive attack expectations over the triggering threshold for launch on warning. The error would inadvertently bring commanders perilously close to the level of certainty presumably required to authorize retaliation. Table 5, for example, shows that an initial expectation of 40 percent would jump to 86 percent (0.857) on the basis of a single positive indication of attack, while the assumed type II error rate (10 percent) generates this indication by mistake once every ten readings (once every fifty minutes).

In contrast, piloted aircraft, and to a lesser extent cruise missiles, give more ambiguous warning information that is more difficult to interpret even if it is reliably received. As partial compensation, the relatively slow speeds of these systems allow more decision time and thus more cycles of judgment than ballistic missiles do. But, as suggested by tables 7 and 8, that allowance could present problems of a different sort. If stealthy aerodynamic threats in effect increase the error rate of the warning system—let us suppose error rates of 25 percent compared with 10 percent for ballistic missiles, recognizing the less ambiguous warning associated with missiles—then the result is a sluggish convergence of judgment on detection of attack not only due to Bayesian logic, which revises judgment in smaller increments as the error rate increases, but also due to the greater incidence of negative readings mixing in with positive readings to muddy the picture. (The effect of negative reports on prior expectations is shown in table 8 for a warning system with assumed error rates of 25 percent, and in table 6 for error rates of 10 percent.) A sequence of positive and negative readings might trap the decision process in a cycle of estimates that remain in the midranges of subjective probability. The process does not readily converge on any judgment clear enough to support a decision on retaliation.

At the same time the process does not allow for a rapid downward adjustment of expectations when an attack is *not* under way. There are ample opportunities for false alarms to appear, given a type II error rate of 25 percent, and substantial scope for repetitive false indications. While the decision process would usually become trapped in the midranges of subjective probability, there is a significant risk of successive false alarms that would drive expectations to dangerous levels, though still below the triggering threshold for launch on warning. Table 7, for example, shows that an initial expectation of 40 percent would jump to 67 percent (0.667) in one cycle with positive indication and to 86 percent (0.857) in two cycles that each have positive indications. Given the assumed type II error rate of 25 percent, the repetitive false positives that elevate expectations to 86 percent have a significant chance of appearing. This likelihood is 6 percent (25 percent × 25 percent). By comparison, recall that expectations rise from 40 percent to 86 percent on the basis of a single false positive when the assumed type II error rate is 10 percent, and that the chance of this happening in one cycle of judgment is 10 percent.

The difficulty of Bayesian convergence is also exacerbated in an attack sequence that does not begin massively and that includes partial damage to sensors. At the onset of the attack, an intact warning system might provide a strong indication of attack, particularly ballistic missile attack, but only weak, preliminary indications of its size and objective. With the onset of damage to sensors, the system might be unable to confirm the initial strong indication, assess the character of the initial salvo, or detect follow-on raids by other forces.[10] These circumstances could initially produce the rapidly converging judgment characteristic of a good (low error rate) warning system followed by the slowly converging or nonconverging process characteristic of a poorer (high error rate) system after the sensors are damaged. If the command system is not prepared to take damage to warning sensors as decisive evidence of a full-scale strategic attack, then its internal decision process would be in considerable difficulty. If it does react decisively on that evidence alone, it would make itself prone to type II errors.

Case 2

If subjective confidence vested in the tactical warning system is *not* lowered despite an actual degradation in the system's error rates, then the expectations of attack are overdetermined by tactical information. Bayesian computations that continue to be based on the assumption of a good (low error rate) warning system after the transition to crisis circumstances that drastically reduce warning performance cause expectations to shift more sharply than is actually warranted. The consequences of these excessive adjustments are either very fortuitous or very unfortunate, depending on the actual state of nature.

Figure 1 shows that this overdetermined process works to the advantage of a rapid reaction posture under conditions of actual enemy attack. The graph displays several curves, one of which (curve a) represents the changes in expectations that follow receipt of positive attack indications when the subjective confidence vested in the warning system corresponds to peacetime error rates. The other curves (b and c) represent the revision of expectations when the subjective confidence vested in the system is reduced to various levels (alternatively 0.1 and 0.25). They clearly show that overrating the performance level of tactical warning systems facilitates rapid convergence on the correct judgment in the circumstance of actual attack. The overrating fortuitously bolsters the feasibility of executing, for example, a classic launch-on-warning response.

The effects of overrating the system are the opposite of fortuitous, however, if an attack is not under way. A single false positive alarm (whose probability could be as high as 25 percent) catapults expectations of attack to near certitude, as curve a of figure 1 shows, instead of raising it to the lower levels displayed in curves b and c.

**Figure 1. Initial and Revised Expectations of Attack Given
Attack Warning**

A. Initial Estimate = 0.01′   B. Initial Estimate = 0.20′

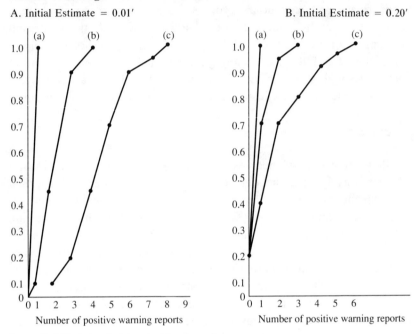

Number of positive warning reports   Number of positive warning reports

Degree of belief in the hypothesis "an attack is under way":
   (a) assuming a warning system with 5 percent type I and 0.0001 type II error rates;
   (b) assuming a warning system with 10 percent types I and II error rates;
   (c) assuming a warning system with 25 percent types I and II error rates.

Gross misinterpretation of tactical information thus results from vesting
unwarranted confidence in the performance of the warning system.

Because rapid operational reactions of strategic forces sharply limit
the amount of tactical data available for use in testing the hypothesis
"an attack is under way," the randomness inherent in the frequency
distributions associated with types I and II errors has an opportunity
to play a dangerously mischievous role in Bayesian inference. Probabilities stabilize as sample size increases, as every statistician knows. A
small sample of trials, whether readings from a warning system or flips
of a coin, invites a run of bad luck. Flip a fair coin a hundred times,
and the result is a pretty even distribution of heads and tails. Flip it a
couple of times, and the result may easily be all heads or all tails. We

cannot count on the results of a coin-flipping experiment to approximate the theoretical distribution unless the sample size is large.

Similarly, the types I and II error rates of the tactical warning system tend over the short run to deviate from their long-run rates. A system with a type I error rate of 10 percent, for instance, will detect an attack about 90 percent of the time when tested over a large number of trials. The experimental results will approximate the central tendency—the expected value of the theoretical distribution—if sufficient tests are conducted. But the distribution over a small number of trials tends to be more scattered. A detection failure on the first or second reading, or both readings, of the tactical warning output would defy the odds but would not violate stochastic sense. Such a failure rate cannot persist over dozens of readings without shocking statistical laws, but its initial appearance would come as no great surprise to the theory of probability.

Monte Carlo simulation techniques can be applied to explore the possibilities for unusual distributions to manifest themselves on a given trial run. In this technique, a random number generator determines whether an attack indication is present $(+)$ or absent $(-)$. This determination is made for each of two scenarios: a scenario of attack (case 1) and a scenario of no attack (case 2). For each scenario, the random number generator in effect blindly selects a symbol from an imaginary urn containing $+$ and $-$ symbols. For the attack scenario (case 1), the proportion of $+$ and $-$ symbols in the urn corresponds to the assumed type I (detection failure) error rate of the tactical warning system. If the type I error rate is assumed to be 10 percent, for example, then the ratio of $+$ to $-$ symbols in the urn is 9:1. The random number generator is thus likely to pluck a $+$ (attack indication) from the urn, but it might pluck a $-$ (no attack indication) instead. This pick would be unlucky in that scenario (attack). For the no attack scenario (case 2), the proportion of symbols in the urn corresponds to the assumed type II (falsely detected attack) error rate. If the type II error rate is assumed to be 10 percent, for example, then the ratio of $+$ to $-$ symbols in the urn is 1:9. The random number generator is thus likely to pluck a $-$ (no attack indication) from the urn, but it might pluck a $+$ (attack indication) instead. This pick would be unlucky in that scenario (no attack).

**Figure 2. Bayesian Updating of Attack Expectations,
One Typical Trial Run**

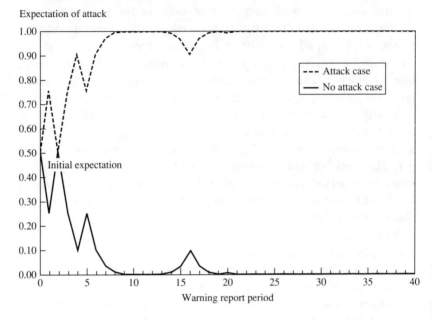

Expectation of attack

One can then apply the Bayesian inference model to the randomly selected "events." When a + is picked from the urn, the model selects the posterior probability associated with the presence of attack warning. When a − is picked, it selects the posterior probability associated with the absence of attack warning. In either event, the model replaces the original prior probability with the appropriate posterior, which becomes the new prior for a second cycle of readings and judgments. This cyclic process continues under both hypothetical scenarios until Bayesian computations converge on the proper judgment—that is, until the posterior expectation of attack rises to 100 percent for the attack scenario and drops to 0 percent for the no attack scenario. A single trial run of the model is displayed as repetitive calculations of the subjective expectation of attack for each of the separate cases.

Figure 2 is an example of a trial run when the model parameters assumed a prior probability of 50 percent and a type I and type II error rate of 25 percent. Despite the relatively high error rate of the tactical warning system, the iterative revision of expectations using Bayes's

Figure 3. Bayesian Updating of Attack Expectations, One Atypical Trial Run

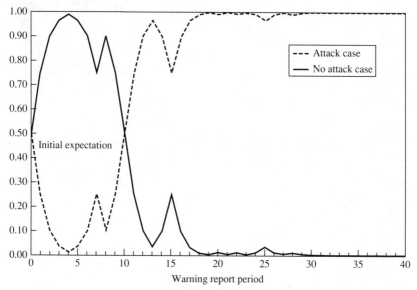

Expectation of attack

Warning report period

theorem gradually but inexorably converges on the correct final judgment in both cases. The number of judgment cycles needed to get there is quite large, far exceeding the small number of readings of tactical warning output allowed by the current rapid reaction posture of strategic forces.

With the same parameters, the model produced the results displayed in figure 3 on another trial run. Compared with other trial runs using these settings, the results are atypical. (Figure 2 is a typical set of results.) They are nonetheless illuminating for showing the short-run instabilities of a stochastic process. The early odds-defying readings from the tactical warning system brought Bayesian commanders to the brink of fatal misjudgment before the process settled down. A subjectively rational process of logical inference temporarily suffered from erratic warning performance. A streak of bad luck afflicted the warning system, which in turn fed incorrect data into the hopper of Bayesian logic. This pattern substantiates the point that subjectively and objectively warranted degrees of belief do not necessarily coincide.

Figure 4. Bayesian Updating of Attack Expectations, Average over Forty Trial Runs

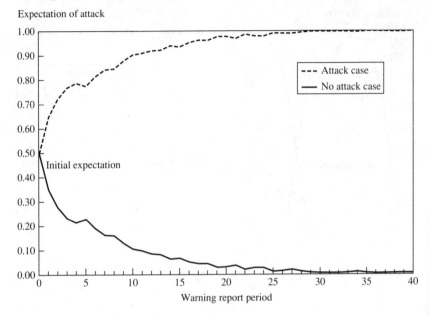

We ran the model many times using the same parameters, and for each trial recorded the serial adjustments of posterior probabilities as they gravitated toward 0 or 100 percent. We then computed the average posterior expectation across all the trial runs each time the model received a warning report and revised expectations. Put differently, the posterior expectation after the first cycle of judgment in all the trials was averaged and plotted on a single graph. In like fashion, the average for the second cycle of judgment in all the trials was computed and plotted. And so forth. The total number of trial runs was large enough (forty) to warrant statistical confidence that the computed averages along the curves shown in figure 4 conform to the expected values of the theoretical distribution, though not exactly, because the effects of random chance are still present.

We reran the model using the same error rate parameters but varying the degree of initial expectation of attack. For each different prior probability, the model executed forty trial runs. We then varied the error rate parameters and executed forty trial runs for each of the prior

Table 9. Judgment Errors after Two Warning Periods[a]

Initial estimate[b]	Undetected attack[c]	Falsely detected attack[d]
0.001	40	0
0.1	7	0
0.4	8	1
0.7	5	2
0.9	0	5

a. Assumes a warning system with 5 percent types I and II error rates.
b. Degree of belief in the hypothesis "an attack is under way."
c. Number of times out of 40 trial runs that the final expectation of attack failed to reach 90 percent when an attack in fact occurred.
d. Number of times out of 40 trial runs that the final expectation of attack reached 90 percent when an attack in fact did not occur.

probabilities. As an excursion, the model also ran a series of runs in which the command system assumed error rates that were lower than those actually achieved by the warning system.

Some of the results are summarized in table 9, which shows that a command system attuned to the prospect of attack is less likely to miss an attack but is also more susceptible to believing an attack is under way when it is not. As table 10 shows, overvesting confidence in the tactical warning system aggravates this trade-off. The command system becomes less prone to miss an attack, but it pays for this improvement by a greater propensity to detect an attack falsely.

The results are not egregiously alarming, but neither are they

Table 10. Judgment Errors after Two Warning Periods (Unrevised Assumptions)[a]

Initial estimate[b]	Undetected attack[c]	Falsely detected attack[d]
0.001	10	0
0.1	0	7
0.4	3	10
0.8	0	8

a. Assumes a warning system with 10 percent actual types I and II error rates, *but* the command system assumes 5 percent type I and 0.0001 type II error rates.
b. Degree of belief in the hypothesis "an attack is under way."
c. Number of times out of 40 trial runs that the final expectation of attack failed to reach 95 percent when an attack in fact occurred.
d. Number of times out of 40 trial runs that the final expectation of attack reached 95 percent when an attack in fact did not occur.

comfortably reassuring. They suggest, which is all they can do, that
catastrophe is not inevitable even at the appreciable error rates
assumed, but that it is distinctly possible. The chances of it happening
do not build continuously over time, for it is associated with crisis
conditions—that is, a sharp departure from normal peacetime circumstances to which the respective strategic forces have become stably
adapted. How likely are such crises? Not very, we can surmise from
several decades of experience, and even less likely with the recent
improvement in the U.S.-Soviet political relationship. But beyond
these vague suppositions is a harder truth: we simply do not know.

So What?

Since the empirical validity of the Bayesian inference model cannot
be established for the crisis conditions to which it is most sensitive,
the analysis that emerges from it poses a larger question of perspective
and presumption; namely, where should the burden of proof lie? In
the normal practice of science there is a simple, well-established answer
to that question. Any theoretical argument carries the burden of
demonstrating its validity; if a theory is so construed that empirical
demonstration becomes impossible, then the theory is contemptuously
dismissed. In terms of security policy, however, that is not an
acceptable standard. Because of the destructive capabilities of strategic
forces, some judgment must be made about the stability of unexperi-
enced crisis conditions and some theory must be used in making the
judgment. Security requires that any serious flaws in the utilized theory
be discovered before they are proved by decisive experience. Given
that situation, there is a good reason to impose the burden of proof on
anyone who would deny the more somber implications of the Bayesian
model; namely, that strategic force deployments in their current and
projected operational configuration are a fatal accident waiting to
happen.

As a practical matter, of course, the normal scientific standard holds
for reasons that go well beyond the priorities of science. There is a
natural, understandable predilection to believe that at least one's own
strategic forces are safely managed and that ultimate wisdom prevails
in the disposition of such annihilating power. Quite apart from the
question of scientific proof, there is considerable psychological and

political resistance to any perspective that encourages doubt about one's own actions as distinct from doubt about the opponent's. That is part of the subtle danger which modern strategic forces impose. Self-doubt, often the crucible of new insight and illuminating perspective, is powerfully discouraged.

For those, however, who are willing to contemplate the possibility that prevailing strategic security policy may not capture complete and final wisdom, some practical implications of the Bayesian inference model are worth pondering. If it is admitted that the reasonable requirements of deterrence can be accomplished at force deployments far lower than those now prevailing, and if it is further admitted that a viable deterrent effect, even at lower force levels, does not depend on rapidly accomplished destruction or an operational optimization of the sequence of retaliation, then some useful implications emerge.

The commitment to attack opposing strategic weapons that so drives the rapid reaction posture can and should be authoritatively removed from each strategic organization's mission assignments. Cooperative warning arrangements should be developed to improve each warning system's ability to demonstrate that an attack is *not* in progress. The deployments of manned aircraft, particularly those using stealth technology designed to confuse opposing warning systems, should be strictly controlled at modest levels of deployment. Warning system assets should be the focus of greater investment, and explicit arrangements should be made for mutual protection of these assets, most notably an agreement prohibiting deployment of dedicated antisatellite weapons. Command systems should be configured to allow rapid and reliably effective reimposition of central political control over strategic weapons should some crisis circumstances ever trigger the protective dissemination of authority to execute retaliatory missions.

These illustrative implications starkly contradict the current operational planning and procurement commitments of the two major strategic establishments. They indicate that vital elements of strategic security have not yet been mastered.

Notes

1. Michael M. May, George F. Bing, and John D. Steinbruner, *Strategic Arms Reductions* (Brookings, 1988).
2. John D. Steinbruner, "Deterrence after Deep Cuts," *Arms Control Today,* vol. 18 (May 1988).
3. "It is this feature of Bayes' theorem that saves Bayesian statistics from being wholly subjective. Initially subjective opinion is brought into contact with data through the operation of Bayes' theorem, and with enough data, differing prior opinions are made to converge. This comes about because the prior opinions become less and less relevant to posterior opinion as more and more data are observed. Prior opinion is swamped by the data, so that posterior opinion is controlled solely by the data. For a Bayesian, this is the only way in which data can 'speak for themselves.'" L. D. Phillips, *Bayesian Statistics for Social Scientists* (London: Nelson, 1973), pp. 76–78.
4. Our application of Bayes's theorem is as follows:
   Definitions:
   Prob (attack|tactical warning) = $P(A|W)$
   Prob (attack|no tactical warning) = $P(A|NW)$
   Prob (tactical warning|attack) = $P(W|A)$ = 1 − prob (type I error)
   Prob (tactical warning|no attack) = $P(W|NA)$→type II error
   Prob (no tactical warning|attack) = $P(NW|A)$→type I error
   Prob (no tactical warning|no attack) = $P(NW|NA)$ = 1 − Prob
     (type II error)

   Prior initial subjective expectation of an attack: prior (A)
   Posterior subjective expectation of an attack after either receiving or not
     receiving tactical warning: post (A)

   Formulas:
   Given tactical warning is received during warning report period:
   $$\text{Post } (A|W) = \frac{P(W|A)\,\text{prior}(A)}{P(W|A)\,\text{prior}(A) + [P(W|NA)(1 - \text{prior}(A)]}$$
   Given tactical warning is *not* received during warning report period:
   $$\text{Post } (A|NW) = \frac{P(NW|A)\,\text{prior}(A)}{P(NW|A)\,\text{prior}(A) + [P(NW|NA)(1 - \text{prior}(A)]}$$

5. During the tensest phase of the Berlin crisis in the summer of 1961, President Kennedy reportedly remarked that "there was one chance out of five of a nuclear exchange." Arthur M. Schlesinger, Jr., *A Thousand Days: John F. Kennedy in the White House* (Houghton Mifflin, 1965), p. 395. During the Cuban missile crisis of 1962, Kennedy believed, by his own account, that the odds of war were "somewhere between one out of three and even." Theodore C. Sorensen, *Kennedy* (Harper and Row, 1965), p. 705.

6. MITRE Memorandum D40-M247 (June 2, 1989).

7. The implications of the state of internal consensus on the gravity of a crisis extend well beyond the narrow issue of tactical warning interpretation. The way in which national policy and military operations interact is affected. If military organizations fail to understand the assessments, expectations, and intentions of national policy officials, then their precautionary alert operations may not be properly aligned with the way in which the core security problem has been framed by the apex of government. Successful efforts on the part of national leaders to set the expectations of military organizations nevertheless by no means ensure, but only facilitate, consistency between national policy and the diffuse military response to crisis circumstances. In a comparative analysis of the Cuban missile crisis and the 1973 Middle East conflict, Steinbruner found that national officials managed to set a general political construction on the course of events that shaped the alert operations undertaken by attentive U.S. military organizations, but that certain military actions clearly diverged from the intent of national leaders during the Cuban episode. John D. Steinbruner, "An Assessment of Nuclear Crises," in Franklyn Griffiths and John C. Polanyi, eds., *The Dangers of Nuclear War* (University of Toronto Press, 1979), pp. 34-49.

8. An argument can be made that certain types of strategic warning are *not* more ambiguous and less reliable than tactical warning indications. For instance, communications intercepts revealing the dissemination of enemy launch instructions are arguably less ambiguous than blips on a radar screen indicating missiles in flight.

9. This calculation of unsuccessful adaptation is based on formulas used by Ashby to illustrate the probability of successful adaptation by complex systems. The points of our illustrations are exactly the opposite, but the math is identical. W. Ross Ashby, *Design for a Brain* (London: Chapman and Hall, 1978), pp. 150-52.

10. The canonical scenario for this degradation involves the launch of a small contingent of submarine ballistic missiles (SLBMs) whose warheads explode at high altitude several minutes later, producing electromagnetic pulse effects that damage space- and ground-based tactical warning sensors. The initial launch might be detected by an intact warning system, but the subsequent sensor damage might prevent follow-on confirmation and assessment of this precursor attack as well as detection and assessment of any salvo of ICBM forces that follows on the heels of the SLBM launch.